The Glory of the Garden

For the Glory of the Garden glorifieth every one.
- Rudyard Kipling

This book is dedicated to:
All the members, past and present, of
St. Jude's Garden Guild
and especially to
Jean Mullholland and Grace Irvine
who first had the vision of a garden.

The Glory of the Garden

St. Jude's Anglican Church in Oakville

Photographs by Diana Wiggins

The Glory of the Garden:
St. Jude's Anglican Church in Oakville
Rubicon Publishing Inc.
109 Thomas Street, Box 69596
Oakville, Ontario L6J 7R4, Canada

Canadian Cataloguing in Publication Data
Wiggins, Diana
The glory of the garden:
St. Jude's Anglican Church in Oakville

ISBN 0-921156-61-8

1. Church gardens — Ontario — Oakville — Pictorial works,
2. St. Jude's Anglican Church (Oakville, Ont.) — Pictorial works.
I. Title.

Designed by Catherine Chatterton

Printed and bound in Hong Kong

Table of Contents

On a sunny day in the spring, summer, or autumn, passersby walking along William Street in Oakville — a beautiful town situated on the shores of Lake Ontario — will come upon a garden that will make them stop in wonder. It is the garden of St. Jude's Anglican Church.

This is the story of the garden, and of the group of dedicated volunteers who created it and keep it growing.

It is also the story of all gardens — of the cycle that unfolds each year from bud to blossom to "withered sere" and then to bud again.

The nature of God is a circle of which the centre is everywhere and the circumference is nowhere.

- Source unknown, possibly Empedocles

Creating the Garden

And they shall say, This land that was
desolate is become like the garden of Eden.
    - *Ezekiel 36:35 (King James' Bible)*

St. Jude's Anglican Church began its life as a mission in 1839, in a log cabin on the banks of the Sixteen Mile Creek. Oakville was then a small village of 500 people. Between 1842 and 1884, worship services were held in a frame building at the corner of Lakeshore Road and Thomas Street. The church moved into its present home on William Street in 1884. Today, St. Jude's serves a congregation of approximately 800 families.

For close to a century, the church grounds remained a bare stage — a field of dandelions where church picnics were held and rugby and football matches were played. In the early 1980s, Canon Ian Dingwall, then Rector, developed an idea for the creation of a memorial garden for the interment of the ashes of deceased parishioners. John Simkins started the process by planting a flower bed along the west side of the church.

The Memorial Garden

The transformation of the property really began in 1982, when parishioner Jean Mulholland helped establish a formal, enclosed garden in memory of her late husband, Peter Mulholland.

Wrapped within a low brick wall and wrought iron gate, the Memorial Garden featured a "tree of life" fountain and a sundial sitting on intricate brickwork bordered all around by flower beds. The new garden brought a dramatic change to the church grounds. Jean and her friend Grace Irvine, both ardent gardeners, were delighted with the results and decided to extend the development of the garden to the entire property.

You have a garden walled around
Chosen and made special ground;
A little spot enclosed by grace,
Out of the world's wide wilderness.

          - Isaac Watts (1674 - 1748)

St. Jude's Garden Guild

Jean and Grace recognized that they were embarking on a project that was too big for them to handle by themselves. At a Sunday service in the spring of 1983, Grace described their vision of a garden on the property, and she invited avid gardeners in the congregation to help make it happen. Six people met with her in the church kitchen after the service, and the St. Jude's Garden Guild was formed.

Some of the Guild members still remember the toil of the early years. With almost no funds, the volunteers brought their own tools to clean up the grounds. They trimmed overgrown hedges and removed piles of garbage. They tore down an old shed, pulled out a collapsed fence, and even filled in a ditch. Finally, they were ready to begin planting a garden.

A garden never looks perfect; something is always dying, something about to bloom.

Nigel Nicolson (son of Vita Sackville-West and Harold Nicolson) 1993

Grace laid out the design for the garden and the first flower beds were dug and filled with plants from the Guild members' own gardens. As a result, the early beds were a real "hodge podge" according to Grace. When more plants were needed, parishioners began the tradition of donating shrubs and trees as memorial gifts. Slowly and steadily a garden began to emerge.

Today, a magnificent perennial garden stands in place of the dandelion field. Tulips and hyacinths, rhododendrons and peonies, roses, irises, foxgloves, and many more beautiful flowers bloom where weeds once flourished.

Every Thursday — whether sunny or drizzly — the dedicated volunteers arrive and spend three hours tending to their own section of the garden. Mid morning, they take a short break to share a coffee and confer on matters of the garden. "Those coffee breaks are our only meetings all through the gardening season," said Grace Irvine.

Your work, O God, needs many hands...
*   - Calvin Weiss Laufer (1874 - 1938)*

And when your back stops aching
and your hands begin to harden,
You will find yourself a partner
in the Glory of the Garden.

       - Rudyard Kipling (1865 - 1936)
         from "The Glory of the Garden"

Oh Adam was a gardener,
and God who made him sees
That half a proper gardener's work
is done upon his knees.

  - Rudyard Kipling (1865-1936)
    from "The Glory of the Garden"

Fundraising for the Garden

The Garden Guild holds a plant and compost sale each spring to raise funds for the maintenance and improvement of the garden. These fundraising efforts have made it possible for the Guild to purchase plants, major gardening equipment, and an automatic sprinkler system.

On the day of the plant sale, another group of parishioners also holds a sale of annuals for the benefit of various charitable projects. The geraniums, impatiens, and petunias make a spectacular display on the church lawn.

The annual plant sale at St. Jude's is a much anticipated event that always draws a large crowd. Eager gardeners wait in line before the sale begins and plants are bought and swiftly carted away once the doors open. For many people in the community, the St. Jude's plant sale is the start of their gardening season.

The Garden Chapel

During a sabbatical in 1997, Canon Alex Hewitt, the current Rector, toured the Holy Land where he saw many outdoor chapels and gardens. At the Garden of Gethsemane, he was struck with the idea of an outdoor chapel for St. Jude's. Following many discussions, the congregation approved the idea and landscape architect Dan Tregunno donated the plans for the new chapel. Once again, family memorials and gifts brought the idea to reality. The Garden Chapel was consecrated by Bishop Ralph Spence in August 2000.

The Garden Chapel commemorates the gardens of Biblical stories. Textual inscriptions and artwork reflect the Garden of Eden, the Garden of Gethsemane, and the Garden of the Resurrection.

The chapel was designed to be an inviting place to sit and enjoy the gardens as well as a place of meditation. Outdoor weddings are conducted there, as well as outdoor Eucharists and St. Francis' Day Blessing of Animals.

Through the dim aisles the sunlight penetrates,
And nature's self rejoices; heaven's light
Comes down into my heart, and in its might
My soul stands up and knocks at God's own
temple-gates.

> - Charles Sangster (1822 - 1893)
> "Sonnets, Written in the Orillia Woods"

God who touchest earth with beauty,
make my heart anew;
with thy Spirit recreate me
pure, and strong, and true.

> - Mary Susannah Edgar (b. 1889)

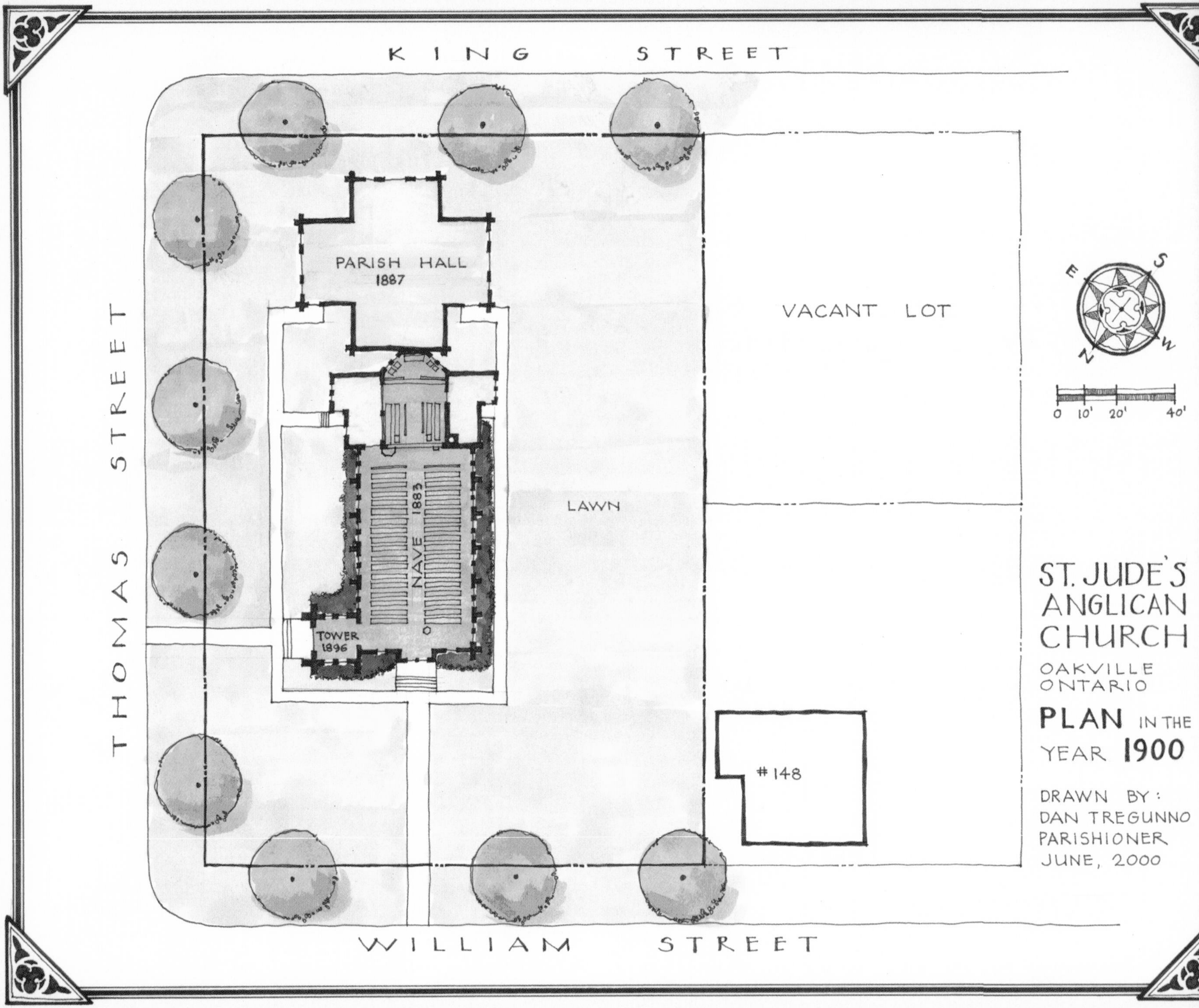

KING STREET

THOMAS STREET

PARISH HALL
1887

NAVE 1883

TOWER
1896

LAWN

VACANT LOT

#148

WILLIAM STREET

E S
N W

0 10' 20' 40'

ST. JUDE'S
ANGLICAN
CHURCH
OAKVILLE
ONTARIO

PLAN IN THE
YEAR 1900

DRAWN BY:
DAN TREGUNNO
PARISHIONER
JUNE, 2000

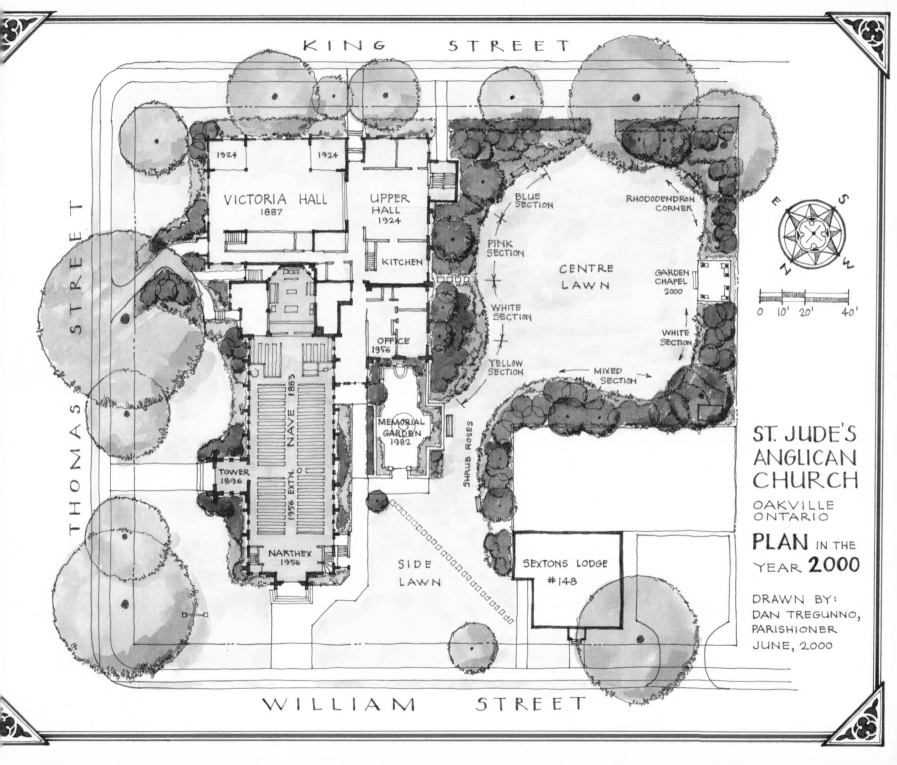

KING STREET

THOMAS STREET

1924   1924

VICTORIA HALL
1887

UPPER
HALL
1924

KITCHEN

OFFICE
1956

NAVE 1883

1956 EXTN.

TOWER
1896

MEMORIAL
GARDEN
1982

NARTHEX
1956

SHRUB ROSES

BLUE
SECTION

PINK
SECTION

WHITE
SECTION

YELLOW
SECTION

CENTRE
LAWN

RHODODENDRON
CORNER

GARDEN
CHAPEL
2000

WHITE
SECTION

MIXED
SECTION

SIDE
LAWN

SEXTONS LODGE
#148

E
S
N
W

ST. JUDE'S
ANGLICAN
CHURCH

OAKVILLE
ONTARIO

PLAN IN THE
YEAR 2000

DRAWN BY:
DAN TREGUNNO,
PARISHIONER
JUNE, 2000

0   10'   20'   40'

WILLIAM STREET

Enjoying the Garden

There is a garden where our hearts converse,

At ease beside clear water, dreaming

A whole and perfect future for yourself,

Myself, our children and our friends.

-Theo Dorgan (b. 1953)

from "The Promised Garden"

The garden of St. Jude's Church is a colourful haven that is used and enjoyed by parishioners and members of the Oakville community. The garden is a scenic setting for picnics, concerts, art exhibitions, and other fundraising events. It has also been featured in garden tours organized by the Oakville Horticultural Society.

Not wholly in the busy world, nor quite
Beyond it, blooms the garden that I love.
*   - Alfred, Lord Tennyson (1809-1892)*
*   from "Suburban Garden"*

As soon as weather permits, many activities take place in the garden. Coffee and lemonade are served on the lawn each Sunday after service.

Most Saturdays, bridal parties can be seen posing for photographs in the different sections of the garden.

Throughout the season, visitors come by every day to admire the flowers or just to relax on the benches set invitingly around the property.

Here at the fountain's sliding foot,
Or at some fruit tree's mossy root,
Casting the body's vest aside,
My soul into the boughs does glide.
> - Andrew Marvell (1621 - 1678)
> from "The Garden"

Lord Jesus hath a garden, full of flowers gay,
Where you and I can gather nosegays all the day:
There angels sing in jubilant ring,
With dulcimers and lutes,
And harps, and cymbals, trumpets, pipes,
and gentle, soothing flutes.
> - Dutch Hymn (1633)

A Year

in the

Garden

Thus the Seer,
With vision clear,
Sees forms appear and disappear,
In the perpetual round of strange,
Mysterious change
From birth to death, from death to birth,
From earth to heaven, from heaven to earth;
Till glimpses more sublime
Of things, unseen before,
Unto his wondering eyes reveal
The Universe, as an immeasurable wheel
Turning forevermore
In the rapid and rushing river of Time.
- Henry Wadsworth Longfellow (1807 - 1882)
from "Rain in Summer"

For the members of the Garden Guild, the gardening season begins around late March or early April with a meeting to make plans for the year. According to Grace Irvine, the garden was designed "to look after itself" and does not require too much maintenance. Still, the Guild members are kept busy throughout the gardening months.

The first mild days bring the gardeners out for spring clean-up — the debris from winter is raked and removed to allow the early shoots to emerge. Snowdrops push through the retreating frost and are quickly followed by the other bulbs. Almost overnight the anticipation ends — trees are covered in pale new leaves and spring blossoms burst into glory. The Garden Guild begins to prepare for its plant sale in May.

What stands in this garden
is there because I measured, placed, reached
down into the soil and pulled out
stems, leaves, gradually...

- Margaret Atwood (b. 1939)
"Two Gardens"

All summer long, the perennial garden is a stage of many colours. The Guild members continue to tend to it every Thursday morning. Although they work at their own sections, the gardeners regularly share ideas about the garden. They take care to ensure that the individual patches do not form a crazy quilt but instead blend seamlessly into one stunning work of art.

Before anyone is ready for it, the first leaves turn yellow and red, the last blooms fade, and the gardeners' tasks turn to preparation for the approaching winter. Plants that spread out in the summer are divided, overgrown twigs are pruned, and vulnerable plants are covered in protection. Finally, the fallen leaves are raked and removed, and the garden tools are packed away.

The Garden Guild holds its final meeting in November to close the year.

A Gard'ner's work is never at an end; it begins with the Year and continues to the next.

- John Evelyn
The Gardener's Almanac, 1664

Spring
in the
Garden

The year's at the spring,
And day's at the morn;
Morning's at seven;
The hillside's dew-pearled;
The lark's on the wing;
The snail's on the thorn;
God's in his heaven;
All's right with the world.

        - Robert Browning (1812 - 1889)

            from "Pippa Passes"

Whether we look, or whether we listen,

We hear life murmur, or see it glisten;

Every clod feels a stir of might,

An instinct within it that reaches and towers,

And groping blindly above it for light,

Climbs to a soul in grass and flowers;

The flush of life may well be seen

Thrilling back over hills and valleys;

- James Russell Lowell (1819 - 1891)
    from "The Vision of Sir Launfal"

I remember long veils of green rain
Feathered like the shawls of my grandmother —
green from the half-green of the spring trees
Waving in the valley.

- Dorothy Livesay (1909 - 1996)
from "Green Rain"

This is my Father's world;
And to my listening ears
All nature sings and round me rings
The music of the spheres.

This is my Father's world,
I rest me in the thought
Of rocks and trees, of the skies and seas,
His hand the wonders wrought.

This is my Father's world;
The birds their carols raise;
The morning light, the lily white,
Declare their maker's praise.

This is my Father's world;
He shines in all that's fair;
In the rustling grass
O hear him pass,
He speaks to me everywhere
            -Rev. Maltbie D. Babcock (1858 - 1901)

Praise gladly in springtime when earth seems to glow
with new life and colour in all things that grow;
- Edna Fay Grant (b. 1905)
from "Walk Softly in Springtime"

Summer
in the
Garden

Where the bee sucks, there suck I:
in a clowslip's bell I lie;
There I couch when owls do cry.
On the bat's back I do fly
After summer merrily;
Merrily, merrily, shall I live now,
Under the blossom that hangs
on the bough.

        - William Shakespeare (1564 - 1616)

             The Tempest

Here is a brighter garden,
Where not a frost has been;
In its unfading flowers
I hear the bright bee hum;
Prithee, my brother,
Into my garden, come!

  - Emily Dickinson (1830 -1886)

Summer was wealthy with a daze of suntraps,
Daffodil-spitting, sumptuous. Everywhere
Ours for the taking. Whoever has said
It is time to go home is an adult.

Aidan Carl Mathews (b.1956)
from "Woodniche"

One touch of nature makes the whole world kin.

- William Shakespeare (1564 -1616)

Troilus and Cressida

If a seed in the black earth can turn into such beautiful roses, what might not the heart of man become in its long journey toward the stars?

- G. K. Chesterton (1874 - 1936)

My garden all is overblown with roses,
My spirit is all overblown with rhyme...

- Vita Sackville-West (1892-1962)

The Book of Life begins with a man and a woman in a garden.

- Oscar Wilde (1854-1900)

Autumn
in the
Garden

Listen! the wind is rising,
      and the air is wild with leaves,
we have had our summer evenings;
      now for October eves!

                  Humbert Wolfe
                  from "Autumn"

October gave a party;
The leaves by hundreds came —
The Chestnuts, Oaks, and Maples,
And leaves of every name.
The sunshine spread a carpet,
And everything was grand,
Miss Weather led the dancing,
Professor Wind the band.

The Chestnuts came in yellow,
The Oaks in crimson dressed;
The lovely Misses Maple
In scarlet looked their best;
All balanced to their partners,
And gaily fluttered by;
The sight was like a rainbow
New fallen from the sky.

- George Cooper
from "October's Party"

Season of mists and mellow fruitfulness,
Close bosom-friend of the maturing sun;
Conspiring with him how to load and bless
With fruit the vines that round the thatch-eaves run;
To bend with apples the mossed cottage-trees,
And fill all fruit with ripeness to the core;
To swell the gourd, and plump the hazel shells
With a sweet kernel; to set budding more
and still more, later flowers for the bees,
Until they think warm days will never cease,
For Summer has o'er-brimmed their clammy cells.

- John Keats (1795 - 1821).

from "To Autumn"

Winter
in the
Garden

All beautiful the march of days,
as seasons come and go;
The hand that shaped the rose
hath wrought the crystal of the snow;
Hath sent the hoary frost of heaven,
the flowing waters sealed,
And laid a silent loveliness
on hill and wood and field.

- Frances W. Wile (1878 - 1939)
from "All Beautiful the March of Days"

O'er white expanses sparkling pure
the radiant morns unfold;
the solemn splendours of the night
burn brighter through the cold;
life mounts in every throbbing vein,
love deepens round the hearth,
and clearer sounds the angel hymn,
Good will to men on earth.

        - Frances W. Wile (1878 - 1939)
      from "All Beautiful the March of Days"

I love snow, and all the forms
Of the radiant frost;

        - Percy Bysshe Shelley (1792 - 1822)
         from "Rarely, Comest Thou"

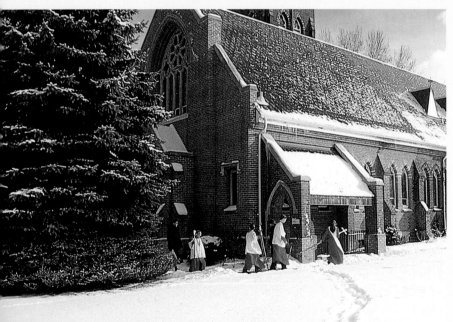

We hear the Christmas angels
The great glad tidings tell;
O, come to us, abide with us,
Our Lord Emmanuel!

- Phillips Brooks (1835-1893)
from "O Little Town of Bethlehem"

If winter comes, can spring be far behind?
- Percy Bysshe Shelley (1792 - 1822)
from "Ode to the West Wind"

A Message from the Rector

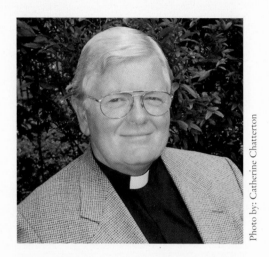

Photo by: Catherine Chatterton

The garden is a place for people, a place for joy and beauty, tears and sorrow, nourishment and peace, rejuvenation and empowerment, miracle and resurrection; people enjoying, working, caring, sharing, creating; people joining with God in the one act of ongoing creation.

May the garden of St. Jude's always be a blessing for you.

- Alex Hewitt, Rector

The Photographer

Photo by: Doug Boult

Diana Wiggins and her husband Don have lived in Oakville for over 30 years. In the early 1980s, Diana successfully completed a certificate course in photography at Sheridan College. Her photographs have been published in numerous trade journals and corporate brochures.

To my husband Don — thank you for your unfailing support, counsel, and patience throughout this project.

St. Jude's Anglican Church gratefully acknowledges the generous support
of the following in our pre-publication sales campaign:

Christopher Invidiata - Invidiata Team RE/MAX aboutowne realty corp.

———

Tim Godfrey - Scotia McLeod

———

Helen Barker - Royal LePage Real Estate Services Ltd.

Michael Caine - CHWO 1250 Radio

Anell Francis - Coldwell Banker Real Estate

Diana Wiggins

———

St. Jude's gives special thanks to Diana Wiggins
and all who inspired the creation of this book.
We thank the various committees and our beloved gardeners.
We offer special thanks to Maggie Goh and Catherine Chatterton
at Rubicon Publishing for their generous support and assistance.

St. Jude's Garden Guild

Present Members

		Past Members
Doreen Botterell	Jean Mulholland	Monica Barrett
Valerie Chapman	Mary Noad	Mary Blachford
Irma Crysler	Barbara Robbins	Peggy Chapman
Michael Etherington	David Senst	Mavis Davison
Geoff Grant	Janet Shirley	Joan Elliott
Barbara Gunyon	John Simkins	Marnie Fraser
Dorrie Hall	Allan Smith	Christine MacLimont
Grace Irvine	Bob Stone	Ellen Oldfield
Jeff Jarvis	Trish Wiltshire	Curzon Ostrom
Beryl Jones	Joan Wright	Wendy Stasiuk
Joan McCallum		Heather Sullivan
Bill McGaw		Susan White
		Joan Woolford

Members of the Garden Book Committees

Susan Ambrose	Irma Crysler	Eileen McCaffrey
Ruth Boughner Idler	Tim Godfrey	John Macdonald
Andrew Brockett	Alex Hewitt	Bob Stone
Sharon Campbell	Julie Hudak	Peter Trahair
Bob Clark	Jeff Jarvis	Dan Tregunno
		Diana Wiggins

And the Glory of the Garden it shall never pass away!
- Rudyard Kipling

All net proceeds from the sale of this book
are being directed to
St. Jude's Outreach Committee
in support of local relief efforts.